100

THINGS TO DO IN
ST. LOUIS
BEFORE YOU
DIE

Old Courthouse dome
Credit: David Lancaster

100

THINGS TO DO IN
ST. LOUIS
BEFORE YOU
DIE

2nd Edition

AMANDA E. DOYLE

REEDY PRESS

Library of Congress Control Number: 2017934711

ISBN: 9781681061221

Design by Jill Halpin
Cover photo: David Lancaster

Printed in the United States of America
17 18 19 20 21 22   5 4 3 2

Please note that websites, phone numbers, addresses, and company names are subject to change or cancellation. We did our best to relay the most accurate information available, but due to circumstances beyond our control, please do not hold us liable for misinformation. When exploring new destinations, please do your homework before you go.

DEDICATION

To Brian, Milo, and Molly, who make every "to-do"
list an adventure

CONTENTS

• •

● ●

Culture and History

• •

● ●

Neighborhoods/Places

• •

PREFACE

I'm a list-maker by nature: I've been known to go back and retroactively write things on my to-do list *after* having done them—just to get that satisfaction of crossing them out. In fact, that's a bit of illumination for how this second edition of a best-selling book came about—realizing that some of the exhilarating additions to my personal St. Louis fun list warranted a spot on an ever-evolving bucket list for this fascinating town.

If I devote even part of every week from now on to exploring the interesting and important corners of St. Louis, I'm seasoned enough to realize that I'll never get to it all. That's another way of saying I'm getting older, and time is flying by. But it's job security for one whose professional and personal interests lie in advocating for the delights, mysteries, and potential of this grand old Midwestern city.

In the preface to the first edition, I pointed out that this isn't "the 100 best places in St. Louis," or even "100 things you have to do"; I'm not here to judge the quality of your explorations! But the items on this idiosyncratic itinerary, when taken as a whole, will offer you a well-rounded St. Louis education. These suggestions will, I hope, give you a new or renewed appreciation for what we have. St. Louis is such an easy city to inhabit, in many ways, and its ease can look deceptively like languor if you don't remember to keep your eyes and ears open.

Approach the list in whatever way makes sense to you: start at the front and go to the back, or dip in and out as your schedule allows. Suggested itineraries and lists of activities organized by season at the back of the book can give guidance if you like a roadmap. Join me and other readers on Facebook (100ThingsSTL) to report back on what you discover. And let me know what has made it onto your list that I should put on mine!

Amanda E. Doyle

Climatron at Missouri Botanical Garden
Credit: David Lancaster

ACKNOWLEDGMENTS

My sincerest thanks to everyone who answered my emails when I wanted to beg/borrow/steal a photograph, but most especially to my former boss, David Lancaster. And my true appreciation is extended to the dozens of *100 Things* city authors who have come after me, for innovative ideas and for keeping this concept flourishing so we can inspire readers together!

Salt + Smoke
Credit: Amanda Doyle

FOOD AND DRINK

BEER ME
AT ANHEUSER-BUSCH

Been on the free Anheuser-Busch tour? If not, do that first. OK, now we're all caught up and ready for the premium experience. For $35, upgrade to the Beermaster Tour, which takes aficionados into the fermentation cellars, the historic Brew House, the Clydesdale Stable & Tack Room, a packaging/bottling line, and private VIP tasting room, post-tour. (Those age 13 to 20 can come along for $15; no one under 13 can enjoy this particular tour flavor, though there's plenty for the kids to do on other tours.) You'll also get some nifty A-B swag to take home, along with a certificate of Beermaster completion, suitable for framing and hanging next to any other earned diplomas on your wall. And while you're encouraged to know your limits, it's worth mentioning the free tastings at the end are unlimited, and the tour itself includes a chug of beer straight out of one of the stainless steel finishing tanks.

1 Busch Place, www.anheuser-busch.com

TIP
So over the world's largest brewer? Well, you're in the right city for that, too. With more than 35 craft breweries fully operational, it's the perfect time to branch out and sample the microbrew taps.
A few recommendations to get you started:

The Civil Life Brewing Co.

Among the most relaxed pubs in town, also offering gourmet snacks and an in-house library
3714 Holt Ave., cash only
www.thecivillifebrewingcompany.com

4 Hands Brewing

Big, bold, flavorful beers and tasty food, too
1220 S. 8th St., 314-436-1559
www.4handsbrewery.com

Urban Chestnut Brewing Company

Recent expansions have vaulted them into mega-micro status, with a convivial and massive bierhall (4465 Manchester), a research/tasting bar plus pizzeria (4501 Manchester), and one of the prettiest beer gardens in town (3229 Washington Ave.),
314-222-0143
www.urbanchestnut.com

'CUE IT
UP

Y'all. There is So. Much. Amazing. Barbecue. Happening in this town right now! We're nestled right here kind of between your Memphis and your Kansas City styles, but the STL barbecue scene is racking up accolades all on its own. From local delicacies like crispy snoots (Smoki O's on Broadway is a great place to try them) to the line-out-the-door goodness on trays at SugarFire, we've got a tang going on.

Of course, the pig that launched a thousand joints, Pappy's, is holding strong in Midtown. (Out front, their smokers even sport hometown cred: my favorite is named "Porky LaFarge.") From that renowned line, directly or indirectly, sprang Bogart's, Adam's Smokehouse, Dalie's Smokehouse, and more. The Shaved Duck, Capitalist Pig, and Salt + Smoke all put their distinctive takes on the meat, and serve 'em up in atmospheres just as varied. Vernon's even smokes tofu, for those with a vegetarian in the crowd.

Sugarfire locations include
9200 Olive Blvd., 314-997-2301;
3150 Elm Point Industrial Dr., 636-724-7601;
932 Meramec Station Rd., 636-825-1400;
605 Washington Ave., 314-394-1720,
www.sugarfiresmokehouse.com

Smoki O's, 1540 N. Broadway, 314-621-8180,
www.smokiosbbq.com

Pappy's, 3106 Olive St., 314-535-4340,
www.pappyssmokehouse.com

Bogart's, 1627 S. 9th St., 314-621-3107,
www.bogartssmokehouse.com

Adam's, 2819 Watson Rd., 314-875-9890,
www.adamssmokehouse.com

Dalie's, 2951 Dougherty Ferry Rd., 636-529-1898,
www.dailiessmokehouse.com

The Shaved Duck, 2900 Virginia Ave., 314-776-1407,
www.theshavedduck.com

Capitalist Pig, 2727 S. 12th St., 314-772-1180,
www.capitalistpigbbq.com

Salt + Smoke, 6525 Delmar Blvd., 314-727-0200,
www.saltandsmokestl.com

Vernon's, 6707 Vernon Ave., 314-726-1227,
www.vernonsbbq.com

EXPERIENCE BEER-VANA
AT THE SAINT LOUIS BREWERS HERITAGE FESTIVAL

Roam free under the giant tents with more than a hundred beers, produced by around fifty of the finest local and craft brewers, that are yours for the sampling. From stalwarts to experimental new recipes, you'll get to try ales, lagers, hybrids, and homebrews in a beer-garden-party atmosphere, typically held near the beginning of June. A rare tapping tent is another fun addition to the festivities, which takes place in an afternoon or evening session (tickets sold separately for each) all along the riverfront underneath the Gateway Arch. Live musical entertainment, food from several local food trucks, and a big fireworks display over the Mississippi River (evening session only) makes for a full experience.

Saint Louis Brewers Guild, www.stlbeer.org/events/heritage/

SLURP DOWN A MALT
AT CROWN CANDY

Pretty much every celebrity chef with a TV show has tried it, and they're not better than you! Whether you aim for Crown Candy Kitchen's five-malt challenge or just want to conquer one, your taste buds will thank you. You can always wash it down with a BLT (also a bit of a heart-stopper, barely contained by bread as it is). And should you prevail in the challenge? Your name will join the annals of history, as recorded in plaques on the walls, engraved with the names of heroes who have gone before you. The old-fashioned soda fountain has been in business under the same family's ownership since 1913, and the often-long lines get even longer around candy-giving holidays like Easter and Valentine's Day. The handmade turtles (they're "snappers" here), hash, and caramels are welcome gifts!

1401 St. Louis Ave., 314-621-9650,
www.crowncandykitchen.net

TIP
For a similar-but-different dining experience in the mid-county area, find a seat at Carl's Drive-In, where the milkshakes come in two flavors (chocolate and vanilla), the root-beer float features housemade soda, and your bill will need to be settled up in cash.
9033 Manchester Rd., 314-961-9652

TREAT YOURSELF
AT A DONUT SHOP

This is a family donut shop town, and you'll have a time keeping your BMI down if you survey all the "bests" that neighbors and co-workers will recommend. From the Donut Drive-In (where people wait in line because they're just that good) to O'Fashion (where numerous images of the King smile down beatifically at your selection, thankyuhverymuch), from Eddie's Southtown Donuts (where patrons seem to enjoy the namesake's swagger almost as much as they enjoy his delectable donuts) to the way-old-school glazed goodies at Duke Bakery in Alton, Illinois, well—there's just no excuse to eat chain donuts unless you have to. We're partial to the whole experience at World's Fair Donuts. Peggy (she of the gravity-defying bouffant and quick-as-a-wink mental addition) will keep your order straight in her head, grabbing your fried pie or chocolate long john, milk, and coffee. She'll whip up your total with a stubby pencil while, behind her, husband Terry and son Byron crank out the next batch of dough, something they do seven days a week at the shop started in the 1940s by Terry's father. Most of these shops are cash-only.

For something completely different, check out Strange Donuts in Maplewood: maple and bacon glaze, Captain Crunch cereal-encrusted donuts, and many more. And Vincent Van Doughnut turned its food-truck mojo into not one but two brick-and-mortar locations, the better to stuff fried dough in your face.

Donut Drive-In, 6525 Chippewa St., 314-645-7714

O'Fashion, 5120 Southwest Ave., 314-772-0398

Eddie's, 4701 S. Kingshighway Blvd., 314-832-1200

Duke Bakery, 819 Henry St., Alton, IL, 618-462-2922,
www.dukebakeryinc.com

World's Fair, 904 Vandeventer Ave., 314-776-9975

Strange Donuts, 2709 Sutton Blvd., 314-398-9530,
www.strangedonuts.com

Vincent Van Doughnut, 1072 Tower Grove Ave.,
314-339-5440, and 40 N. Central Ave., 314-899-9500,
www.vincentvandoughnut.com

EXPERIENCE A SLINGER
AT COURTESY DINER

Like Protestant denominations, the details may vary slightly, but most agree: pile a mess of hash browns, breakfast meat, eggs, chili, cheese, and onions on a plate, and you've got yourself a delicacy. Slingers ain't fancy, ergo neither should your surroundings be. Courtesy Diner's three locations sling 'em 24/7, opting for hamburger patties as the protein of choice. Cash is the coin of the realm here....or, amazingly, traveler's checks.

1121 Hampton Ave., 314-644-2600
8000 S. Laclede Station Rd., 314-553-9900
3155 S. Kingshighway Blvd., 314-776-9059
www.courtesydiner.com

TIP
Other slingers of note around town:
Big Ed's Chili Mac's Diner, downtown, is a classic in part because of its delicious homemade chili, 510 Pine St., 314-421-9040.
White Knight Diner, a.k.a. where the movie *White Palace* was filmed, slings a worthy variation, 1801 Olive St., 314-621-5949.
And this will be anathema to purists, but the vegetarian slinger at The Mud House might actually fill you with energy, instead of greasy regret, 2101 Cherokee St., 314-776-6599.

DO THE TWIST
AT GUS'

At Gus' Pretzels, you can stick to the basics (stick pretzels or the iconic pretzel twist), but feel free to branch out if you're not wedded to tradition: you can get brats, salsiccia, and hot dogs hand-rolled inside pretzels, or order party pretzels shaped like baby carriages, the Arch, the Cardinals logo, and more. It's another multi-generational, family-owned business that has held on and thrived by doing one thing exceptionally well! Bring cash. And if you can't make it to the storefront, Gus' vendors are ubiquitous around city park entrances and busy street corners most weekend mornings. They do a brisk business handing brown-bagged stick pretzels through the car windows of St. Louis.

1820 Arsenal St., 314-664-4010,
www.guspretzels.com

TRY A LENTEN
FISH FRY

You're Catholic, and Fridays during Lent are the time to observe the spirit of sacrifice. You're Catholic, and you don't really go in for all that dogma, but you still have to support your parish. You're not Catholic, but you live in a fairly Catholic city, the spirit of community will warm your heart, and hey, you gotta eat! Pack up the kids (they're more than welcome), about $20, and prepare to feast like royalty. Three picks: St. Cecilia Parish, home of the outrageously popular (read: long line) Mexican fish fry, with fish, tacos, chiles rellenos, and a mariachi band; St. Peter Parish, appropriately enough in St. Peters, filling out the menu with frog legs, peel-and-eat shrimp, and baked potatoes; and St. Pius V, which serves on china, has great live music, and boasts some of the most helpful table-clearing kids on the South Side.

St. Cecilia, 5418 Louisiana Ave., 314-351-1318,
www.stceciliaparishstl.org

St. Peter, 221 First Capitol Dr., 636-946-6641,
www.saintpeterchurchandschool.org

St. Pius V, 3310 S. Grand Blvd., 314-772-1525,
www.stpiusv.org

TASTE THE
FROZEN RAINBOW

You've got the grandaddy of frozen custard, Ted Drewes, where warm nights bring out happy throngs who occupy every bench, railing, and tailgate they can find, while munching on TerraMizzou and Cardinal Sin concretes. But plenty of partisans prefer Mr. Wizard's or Fritz's. Annie's and Bobby's (which also books live bands for popular summer concerts) pack 'em in on the Illinois side. It's practically a civic requirement, in Ferguson, to hang out at the Whistle Stop: the business was recently brought back from retirement/closure by new owners from the community, who have high hopes of continuing its traditions.

Seems there's only one fair way to decide on the best,
and that's to sample them all!

Ted Drewes, 6726 Chippewa St., 314-481-2652, and 4224 S. Grand Blvd. (open summer only), 314-352-7376, www.teddrewes.com

Mr. Wizard's, 2101 S. Big Bend Blvd., 314-781-7566, www.wizardcustard.com

Fritz's, 815 Meramec Station Rd., 636-225-8737, www.fritzsfrozencustard.com

Annie's, 245 S. Buchanan St., Edwardsville, IL, 618-656-0289, www.anniesfrozencustard.com

Bobby's, 2525 N. Center St., Maryville, IL, 618-345-3002, www.bobbysfrozencustard.com

The Whistle Stop, 1 Carson Rd., 314-521-1600, www.fergusonwhistlestop.com

DRINK
MISSOURI WINE

At a Missouri winery, of course. Whether you enjoy the sweet stuff that built our historic viticultural district's early reputation, or you want to partake of award-winning Nortons, Chambourcins, Chardonels, or other dry varietals, choose a reputable local vineyard and let them educate your palate. A number of wineries to the south and west of St. Louis have evolved into daytrip-worthy destinations, with restaurants, spas, lodging, and other amenities. And don't fret if your group includes that one guy who doesn't drink wine: many wineries accommodate with some great locally produced beers and spirits, too!

Several wineries delivering a reliably pleasant experience include:

Chandler Hill Winery, with a handsome indoor tasting room and expansive patio, 596 Defiance Rd., Defiance, 636-798-2675, www.chandlerhillvineyards.com

Chaumette Winery, hilltop location, complete with gourmet dining and overnight villas, in the rolling hills of Ste. Genevieve, 24345 State Route WW, 573-747-1000, www.chaumette.com

Stone Hill Winery, the granddaddy in historic Hermann, with tours available of the arched-stone cellars, the state-of-the-art production facility, and the tasting room, 1110 Stone Hill Highway, 800-909-WINE, www.stonehillwinery.com

EAT LEBANESE
WITH THE LORD

One of those "hidden restaurants" that flies right below the radar, the Wednesday buffet line at St. Raymond's Maronite Cathedral attracts a weekly mix of parishioners, politicians, priests, exiles from nearby downtown offices, and more. The vast ballroom setting, with its chandeliers and mirrored walls, imbues the whole experience with a certain gravitas. The Lebanese specialties, cooked up by a crew of ladies (and a few gents) from cafeteria central casting, include authentic kibbi, spinach pie, lentils and rice, and a lavish table of desserts. Recent leaps into the modern world include the arrival of a credit card machine!

931 Lebanon Dr., 314-621-0056

CHILL OUT
AT VENICE CAFÉ

Leave your cares (and credit cards) behind, and enter the parallel relax-iverse that is the patio at the Venice Café. Part hippie hangout, part music venue, part psychedelic mosaic party HQ, the Venice is a staple of St. Louis nightlife. You can tell a lot about a bar by how many folks in the industry are willing to spend their downtime there . . . and here, the answer is, "a lot." The bathrooms—even the bathrooms!—have more personality than some other entire establishments. Sample the jerk chicken, kebabs, and drinks; come by for a band or open mic show; and see if you don't lose track of time.

1903 Pestalozzi St., 314-772-5994,
www.thevenicecafe.com

GET UP ON THE ROOF
AT VIN DE SET

For as much as St. Louisans love to dine and drink alfresco, it's surprising it took so long for more restaurateurs to follow the lead of Vin de Set and open a classy establishment overlooking some scenic part of town. Ponder the mysteries of that and other phenomena while enjoying French-inspired dishes (like escargot, crab beignets, savory crepes, and beef au poivre) and some amazing beverages on the all-season patio or in the soaring space inside. Large-scale, vintage liquor advertisements bring color and punch to the bar, while a weekly Thursday "Tour de France" prix-fixe is just one of the reasons diners become regulars.

2017 Chouteau Ave., 314-241-8989,
www.vindeset.com

SHOP THE STALLS
OF SOULARD MARKET

Any place in business since 1779 must be doing something right: in this case, bringing together vendors of everything from fresh, organic produce to knockoff designer sunglasses. The mini-donuts alone will keep you moving while you ponder meats, cheeses, spices, baked goods, and maybe that pet bunny you've been considering. Grab flowers for your love or a St. Louis-themed gift basket for your hostess at this busy farmers market in the quirky Soulard neighborhood. The real bargain, though? All this people-watching is free. Saturday morning is the best bet for the street musicians, taste testing, and full experience of this largely indoor market. Fun architectural trivia: the building housing the Grand Hall shops was built in 1929, but is modeled on an Italian foundling hospital from 1419!

730 Carroll St., 314-622-4180,
www.soulardmarket.com

GROW exhibit
Credit: Amanda Doyle

Bi-State Ag Map
What we GROW

Missouri

Missouri and Illinois
Commodities

GROWing
YOUR DINNER

For our experience of being right smack-dab in the middle of America's Heartland, breadbasket to the world and all that, we don't spend a lot of time learning about and celebrating our area's agricultural prowess (or problems). Enter the new GROW exhibit at the Saint Louis Science Center, the country's first permanent outdoor exhibit dedicated to agriculture. From pollinators and pesticides to resident chickens and an interactive GROWbot robot, the science behind the most compelling questions in human agricultural activity is made accessible and relevant for visitors. There are crops growing, of course, and a giant combine to explore. When your head's full and you just need to sit and ponder it all, visit the Fermentation Station for a local beer, wine, or snack. It's a visually striking addition to the Science Center: world-renowned architect Gyo Obata designed the centerpiece pavilion, and its prominent location right along the highway guarantees that it will catch your eye. Bring your city kids and let them "milk" a fake cow, but don't be surprised if you end up learning something, too.

5050 Oakland Ave., 314-289-4400,
slscgrow.squarespace.com

FILL UP
THE MARKET BASKET

For the most complete farmers market experience, the weekly Tower Grove Farmers' Market can't be beat. Some of the region's most conscientious and innovative growers, food producers, and even craftspeople bring their wares to the central pavilion area of Tower Grove Park for your shopping (and snacking) pleasure. Figs, tomatoes, wild honey, proper British scones, corn, pumpkins, apples, grass-fed beef, spring lamb, rainbow chard, fresh pasta . . . the list is kind of making me hungry right now. Throw in the free yoga, great live music, and adjacent kiddie pool and playgrounds, and you've got a perfect summer Saturday. Saturdays from May to October, 8 a.m. to 12:30 p.m.

In Tower Grove Park, Center Cross Dr.,
www.tgmarket.org

TIP
Here in the heartland, great growers markets abound.
Enjoy any (or all!) of the following, in season.

Ferguson Farmers' Market, Saturdays, May-October,
20 S. Florissant Rd., 314-324-4298,
www.fergmarket.com

Maplewood Farmers' Market, Wednesday afternoons
April-October (once-monthly winter markets on
Saturdays), 314-241-2337,
www.schlaflyfarmersmarket.com

Kirkwood Farmers' Market, daily
(Sunday and seasonal hours vary by vendor),
150 E. Argonne Dr., 314-822-0084,
www.kirkwoodjunction.com

Land of Goshen Community Market, Saturdays,
mid-May to mid-October,
downtown Edwardsville, IL, 618-307-6045,
www.goshenmarket.org

Clayton Farmers' Market, Saturdays, May-November,
8282 Forsyth Blvd., 314-913-6632,
www.claytonfarmersmarket.com

North City Farmers' Market, Saturdays, June-October,
North 14th St. and St. Louis Ave., 314-241-5031,
www.northcityfarmersmarket.blogspot.com

ELECTRIC
BLUES
LEGENDS

MUSIC AND ENTERTAINMENT

Leroy Pierson at BB's
Credit: Michael Kuelker

FEELS SO GOOD
TO HAVE THE BLUES

That famed St. Louis inferiority complex: you've heard about it, no doubt. How we tend to live in the metaphorical shadow of other, "better" cities and don't do enough to blow our own horns? Well, blow, horns, blow! 2016 saw the opening of the National Blues Museum, a slick and interactive facility devoted to the celebration of the influence of blues music on American and international culture. From the cotton fields of the South to the Great Migration, from the early days of radio to live concerts produced right in the museum's halls, visitors see (and hear) the story of the blues leading right up to today's torch-bearers. We have a wealth of excellent players here (see them most any night on stages around town), and the chance to understand both the genre's complex history and its influence on the jazz/folk/rap/country/rock music of today is unparalleled. Once inside these doors, see installations, enlarged historical photographs, and some important artifacts that guide the way to understanding this poignant and complicated musical style.

615 Washington Ave., 314-925-0016,
www.nationalbluesmuseum.org

SING THE BLUES
AT BB'S

Live music. Every. Single. Night. Not many spots can make that claim, but BB's Jazz, Blues, and Soups lives it, and ups the ante by using their stage and excellent sightlines (to say nothing of the lip-smacking, down-home food, like gumbo, hushpuppies, and sweet potato pie) to showcase the very best in homegrown jazz and blues talent. Booking manager John May was the longtime head of the St. Louis Blues Society, with an unwavering dedication to preserving and promoting the art form. The occasional big-name touring show blows through, too, but nurturing a serious St. Louis scene, with regulars like Bottoms Up Blues Gang, Marquise Knox, and Big George Brock, is their cornbread and butter.

700 S. Broadway, 314-436-5222,
www.bbsjazzbluessoups.com

JUMP, JIVE, WAIL, AND SWING
AT CASA LOMA

Learn how to do any of the above at the Casa Loma Ballroom, a staple for weddings, theme parties, benefit dances, and ticketed events just off Cherokee Street that's been home to folks wanting to shake a tail-feather since the mid-1930s. With a floating dance floor the size of a basketball court, big bands and rockers still grace the stage on weekend nights, with ballroom, rock, and swing dancing opportunities proving to be steady draws. Lessons often precede the full evening's dance card.

3354 Iowa Ave., 314-664-8000,
www.casalomaballroom.com

GET SOUSA-FIED
WITH THE COMPTON HEIGHTS
CONCERT BAND

Old-fashioned (and free!) family entertainment—in the form of marches, show tunes, and singalongs—is enthusiastically delivered by this community ensemble and their frequent guest artists—everyone from Mariachi Los Camperos de Nati Cano to the late Stan Musial, who was an amateur harmonicist. Expect the crowds to really swell for holiday shows including Memorial Day and 4th of July, when patriotism (and sometimes cannon fire) is on full display. Sunday Serenades in Francis Park and Musical Mondays in Tower Grove Park happen June to August at 7:30 p.m. Arrive earlier than that for a good view, and bring your own lawn chair. Concessions are available at the Compton Heights concessions stand in Francis Park.

Francis Park:
St. Louis Hills neighborhood; bounded by Tamm, Eichelberger, Nottingham, and Donovan

Tower Grove Park:
Bounded by Magnolia, Grand, Arsenal, and Kingshighway
http://chband.org/

GET JAZZY
AT THE BISTRO

Turn off your phone and tame your table conversation: Folks come to Jazz at the Bistro to hear the music. If it's been a while since you enjoyed the phenomenon, the early and late sets here—featuring a wide variety of solid players, groups, and vocalists—will be a revelation. It's a reception that wows the performers, too, and they pay it back in spades with enthusiastic endorsements, musical and spoken, from the stage. Major fundraising and a complete re-envisioning of the Bistro space have created more and better ways to enjoy the evening's music. The room has been reoriented to improve sightlines and proximity to the stage, as well as to make the mezzanine more functional. Patrons who want to spend more time chatting than paying strict attention will enjoy the adjacent lounge, where the performance is broadcast onto large screens. And don't forget you can come early and enjoy sophisticated dining, too. Love jazz? You'll love this. Know nothing about jazz? You'll still love this.

3536 Washington Ave., 314-289-4030,
www.jazzstlouis.org

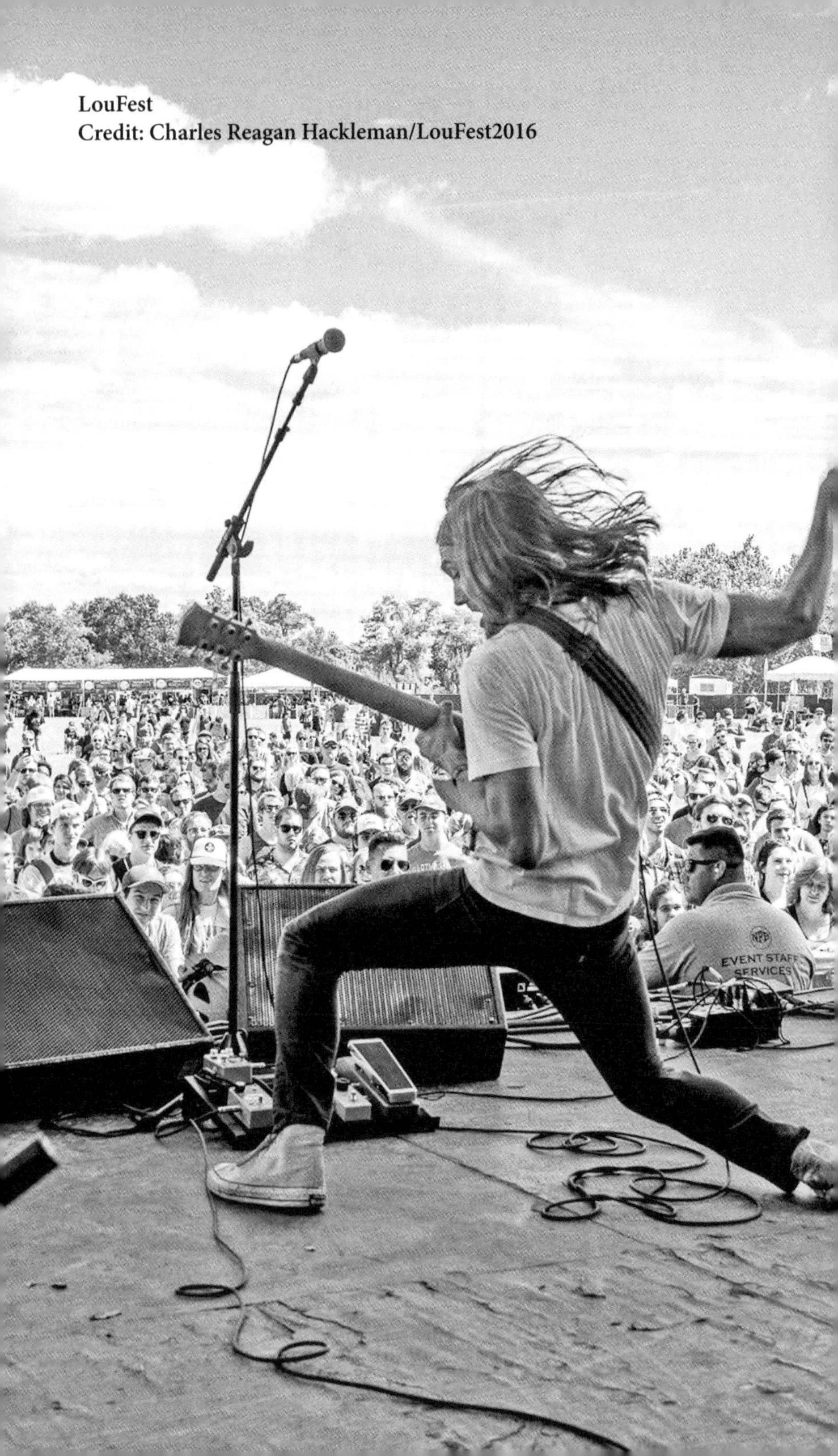

LouFest
Credit: Charles Reagan Hackleman/LouFest2016

ROCK OUT
AT LOUFEST

Once upon a time—the "dark days," as referred to by serious music fans—our town didn't have one of those ginormous, multi-day, outdoor music festivals, the kind where one admission price gets you shows from a wide variety of big-name touring acts. Then along came LouFest to change all that; in fact, it raised the bar. Not only has the Forest Park–based festival brought the Flaming Lips, Jeff Tweedy, Alejandro Escovedo, and Carolina Chocolate Drops to play here, but it's also provided big-crowd exposure for some great local acts. And the scene has remained refreshingly friendly, easy to navigate, locally celebratory (the local food vendors found in the "Nosh Pit" are especially good), and kid-friendly, if that's important to you. Look for consecutive festivals to keep upping the ante, as the fest's reputation continues to be burnished.

September, Forest Park,
www.loufest.com

SOAK UP FREE SUMMER CONCERTS
AT MISSOURI BOTANICAL GARDEN

Right in line with all the rest of our fabulous free attractions, this summer series—from June to August—has fast become a place to hang out with thousands of your nearest and dearest pals. Bring along chairs or a blanket, a picnic dinner (it's one of the few times you can picnic here legally), and a bottle or two of wine. Food and drink are for sale, too, if it's more lugging than you want to do to bring your own. You'll hear some of our town's best musicians in a variety of genres at the Wednesday evening concerts in the Whitaker Music Festival under the stars and amidst the blooming glory of the Garden.

Music starts at 7:30 p.m.
4344 Shaw Blvd., 314-577-5100,
www.missouribotanicalgarden.org

TIP

Bringing the kids? Arrive at 5 p.m., when admission to the grounds is free, and your sprouts can run themselves ragged in the Children's Garden until 7 p.m.

SPEND THURSDAY NIGHT
AT A SNEAKEASY

"Sneakeasy." I just made up that word, but it's an attempt to capture the mix of cool and sly and secret and fun that pervades just about any and everything that goes down on a Thursday evening at Joe's Café & Gallery—two quasi-private spaces next door to each other in the Skinker-DeBaliviere neighborhood. And the best part? Any and everything pretty much describes what you might find. For starters: Thursday nights at the age thirty-plus space are BYOB (or not, depending on what mood the city excise commissioner is in at the moment) and usually feature a smokin' band onstage. Joe's often offers Styrofoam bowls of snacks at the bar or on café tables and always features the wildly eclectic décor you might expect from proprietor and artist Bill Christman. Next door, he curates fantastical gallery shows also open during the Thursday affairs. Outside, he has curated a whole different scene, with a tiki garden, giant heads, and industrial bric-a-brac. One of the city's most unusual, welcoming, and cool-kid scenes.

6014 Kingsbury Ave., 314-862-2541,
www.facebook.com/stlouisjoescafe

FETCH SOME FUN
AT MARDI GRAS

One of Soulard Mardi Gras's best events goes to the dogs—just as it should—on the day of the Barkus Pet Parade and Wiener Dog Derby, held each February or March. Bring your well-behaved (and, if you must, well-costumed) pet, be it pup or parrot, out to stroll the streets, or just come along to gawk at the getups some patient pets will wear. Special attention must be paid to that most amazing process (which you'll see here, undoubtedly), by which some folks start to resemble their pets more than just passingly. And by all means, catch at least one heat of the Dachshund Dash, proof that anyone can develop that champion spirit, even if you're built more along lines of the "low and slow" model.

314-771-5110,
www.mardigrasinc.com

SEE A SHOW
AT THE SHELDON

Renowned far and wide for its acoustics (to say nothing of its handsome, wood-paneled stage and rich stained glass), the Sheldon is a perfect concert experience. Built as the first home for the Ethical Society, it now hosts concerts that often seem like a spiritual experience (unless you're a standard-size-or-above human wedged into the somewhat ascetic balcony seats)! Best bang for the buck is the "Notes from Home" series, featuring local standouts on select weeknights for a lower ticket price. Luminaries of the folk, country, Americana, classical, and singer-songwriter scenes shine bright in this jewelbox of a venue.

3648 Washington Blvd., 314-533-9900,
www.thesheldon.org

DIG UP NEW TUNES
AT VINTAGE VINYL

You don't have to be a hard-core crate digger to get into the groove at Vintage Vinyl. Go in, start with something you already know, and before long, the handmade signage, the multiple listening booths, and the live-mixed, in-store soundtrack will lead you down the rabbit hole of musical discovery. Especially strong, of course, is the selection of recordings by local artists. Outside the store, buskers and other street performers do their earnest best to convince passers-by they're the Next Big Thing. And keep an eye on the marquee and outside walls of the store: they're a catalog of the earthly comings and goings of some of music's luminaries.

6610 Delmar Blvd., 314-721-4096,
www.vintagevinyl.com

WATCH THE WORLD
AT THE ST. LOUIS INTERNATIONAL FILM FEST

Having one of those "sad-to-live-in-flyover-territory" moments? Snap out of it fast at the St. Louis International Film Festival, which takes over screens throughout town for two weeks in November. The best in shorts, features, documentaries, and experimental film from around the world are accessed as easily as falling off a log and into a plush theater seat. It's also an excellent venue for showcasing the best in homegrown talent. Panels, discussions, and parties round out the schedule, and volunteers are always needed—and rewarded. And the presenting nonprofit organization, Cinema St. Louis, offers a plethora of cinematic events year-round, from the LGBTQ-focused QFest to the St. Louis Filmmakers Showcase.

314-289-4151,
www.cinemastlouis.org

LET THE MUSIC PLAY
AT POWELL HALL

You likely already know we have a world-class symphony orchestra, and yet that hasn't been enough to lure you out of the house and into Powell Hall, or it hasn't in a while? Perhaps one of these special events will. Lately, the St. Louis Symphony has taken to playing live scores along with big-screen projections of flicks like *The Matrix, The Wizard of Oz, Harry Potter and the Chamber of Secrets,* and *Pirates of the Caribbean,* to name a few. Want to hear full orchestral oomph behind some of your favorite pop music? Check out concerts devoted to the music of Queen, the Beatles, Whitney Houston, and others. And get your young ones acculturated early, with the terrific one-hour Family Concert matinees designed to engage the kiddos and let them experience live symphonic music without sky-high expectations for complete silence and stillness.

718 N. Grand Blvd., 314-533-2500,
www.stlsymphony.org

Sledding Art Hill
Credit: Brian Marston

SPORTS AND RECREATION

GO ARCH RAVING MAD
FOR THE MISSOURI VALLEY
CONFERENCE

Generally speaking, the attendees at the Arch Madness men's basketball tournament come from outside St. Louis, with fan bases that travel en masse from easy drive-in towns like Carbondale, Wichita, and Des Moines. Sports-savvy locals, though, know that the event has everything you'd want in a college tourney: competing bands, galloping mascots, face-painted cheerleaders, and alumni living and dying with every shot. The basketball played in the Missouri Valley Conference has long been underrated, though their annual crowning of a league champ reminds you that the ball played in the Valley is high-quality hoops, indeed, with worthy theater in the stands and on the sidelines. A rooting interest is preferred but not essential.

First weekend in March, Scottrade Center, 314-444-4300,
www.archmadness.com

SLED
ART HILL

It's so iconic you might think it's overplayed, but it's the kind of hill that sleds, saucers, and even cafeteria trays were meant to glide: Kids of all ages are most welcome to sled down the wide, gentle slope to the Grand Basin from the Saint Louis Art Museum. Sure, you'll have to cruise for parking, and yes, you'll need to pack your own hot chocolate, but the shiny red cheeks and the pictures you'll get, to say nothing of some winter exercise, will be worth it. Remember, downhill skiing rules apply: you're responsible for anyone downhill of you, and you're responsible for ditching if it looks like you're going to break the hay-bale barrier meant to keep you out of the water.

In Forest Park

Nathan Frank Bandstand, Forest Park
Credit: David Lancaster

PADDLE
AROUND THE PARK

Cast off, at least temporarily, from the bustle of Forest Park in a paddleboat built for two, three, or four. You might surprise yourself with how far you can get through the interconnected system of lakes and lagoons, and it won't take long before you can easily spot herons, sunning turtles, and curious ducks. When your legs give out, steam back into port and enjoy lunch or a drink dockside at the Boathouse, where those same curious ducks can get downright grabby when it comes to the last French fry. Boats are first come, first served, and renters must be 18 or older with I.D., though your boat (and supplied life jackets) can accommodate all ages.

6101 Government Dr., 314-367-2224,
www.boathouseforestpark.com

GET BEHIND THE SCENES
AT BUSCH STADIUM

While you're waiting to get called up to the majors, there's an easier way to experience the ambience of a big-league dugout. Daily tours—except on home-day game dates—strike out from the Stan Musial statue at the third base entrance gate to the stadium and take fans to the Cardinals dugout, the Champions Club (home of the World Series trophies), and even the radio broadcast booth, where you can practice your own play-by-play. Make the call. It's a great way to keep Redbird fever stoked even in the off-season, because tours are offered year-round. (And if you need the place all to yourself, for a marriage proposal or to close the business deal, well that's available, too.)

700 Clark St., 314-345-9565,
www.cardinals.com

PLAY LIKE A KING
AT THE ST. LOUIS CHESS CLUB

Ever since philanthropist Rex Sinquefield decided to make it so, St. Louis has evolved into an international hub for chess. Across Maryland Avenue from each other in the Central West End, the World Chess Hall of Fame and the Chess Club and Scholastic Center of St. Louis form the epicenter. Hit up the Hall for changing exhibits related to chess, art, and other intersecting topics, and a terrific gift shop. Want to learn the basics of the game of kings, or looking for a place where there's always someone willing to set up across the board? A membership at the Chess Club is all you'll need, and you may even get facetime with some of the game's visiting luminaries as well.

Chess Club: 4657 Maryland Ave., 314-361-2437,
www.saintlouischessclub.org

Hall of Fame: 4652 Maryland Ave., 314-367-9243,
www.worldchesshof.org

CONVENE
AT THE CONFLUENCE

Where the Mississippi and Missouri rivers swirl together, some of the wildest, widest swaths in the region offer a dizzying array of opportunities to observe, to commune with, and to learn about the natural world. An excellent starting place is the Visitor Center at the Columbia Bottom Conservation Area, the doorway to more than 4,300 acres of trails, marshy wetlands, prairies, bottomland hardwoods, and other native habitats. Maps are available at the Center, and show the location of the hiking, biking, and horseback riding trails, as well as "Exploration Stations" and the public boat ramp which provides access to the Missouri River. Hunting and fishing are permitted in season. The Audubon Center at Riverlands is another worthy stopping-in point: This is heaven for birders, with good populations of waterfowl and shorebirds available for viewing all year round. Eagles can be seen during the fall and winter months. This beautiful conservation area is open daily from sunrise to sunset.

I-270 north to Riverview Dr., then north about 2.5 miles, 314-877-6014, mdc.mo.gov

SET SAIL
ON CREVE COEUR LAKE

Ahoy, landlocked landlubbers! You don't need open water to earn your skipper's bragging rights. Head out to Creve Coeur Lake on alternate Sundays (check the online calendar) for small sailboat races. The action starts late morning, when the sailors arrive with their boats and begin setting up sails and rigging. Novices are more than welcome to lend a helping set of hands, and you may find yourself on the water as a volunteer crew member. If you're fully committed to terra firma, Creve Coeur Memorial Park also has picnicking facilities, athletic fields, an archery course, a golf course, a walking and biking trail around the lake, and a place to rent kayaks near the Lake Front entrance. There is something for everyone at this multi-faceted park.

Marine Ave., near Dorsett Rd., 314-576-7200,
www.sailccsa.com

PUSH PEDALS
AT THE GATEWAY CUP

Labor Day Weekend is not all pork steaks and putting away the summer whites: in Lafayette Square, Benton Park, the Hill, and St. Louis Hills, it's race time. The Gateway Cup series brings professional criterium cycling (that's bicycle racing, for the layperson) to some of the city's prettiest neighborhoods for some heart-pumping straightaways and hairpin turns. Kids get a shot at the action in timed races on the courses, by age group, before the pros—here from all over the country—take over. Plenty of neighbors and businesses along the course get into the fun by turning their front yards and walkways into party patios.

Labor Day Weekend, 314-645-1362,
www.gatewaycup.com

TAKE A
FLOAT TRIP

Choose your speed: steady and sporty (canoe), punctuated equilibrium (rafting), or slow and meandering (inner tube). Choose your spot: the Current, Jacks Fork, Black, Huzzah, and Meramec rivers are among the best nearby. Choose your day: weekdays for smaller crowds/fewer hoosiers, weekends for the full party (and behavior/language you might not want your kids to see just yet). If you've never been floating, most outfitters follow the same basic plan: you choose your distance (usually something you can accomplish in the 3- to 7-hour range), they load you and your tube/life jacket up on a big school bus, and you take a hot, bouncy ride to the put-in point. Slather on the sunscreen, flop into your ride, secure your cooler in its own special tube, and away you go. They'll be there to fetch you at the other end.

TIP
Among the outfitters: Akers Ferry: 573-858-3224,
www.currentrivercanoe.com

Bearcat Getaway: 573-637-2264,
www.bearcatgetaway.com

Huzzah Valley Resort: 573-786-8412,
www.huzzahvalley.com

SETTLE A GRUDGE MATCH
AT SOUTH BROADWAY ATHLETIC CLUB

You'll feel like you're in on the reckoning of a grudge match, from your seat, ringside, at the South Broadway Athletic Club's monthly local wrestling lineup. Outrageous characters (Mike Outlaw, Bolt Brady, and Todd Letterman are but a handful of the regulars) with ongoing complicated narratives, girl fights, chair-breaking—all are included with the price of admission. Hipsters rub elbows with grannies and nine-year-olds as they root for the good guys and verbally lambaste the villains. A bit like low-rent WWE, if you can imagine such a thing. Keep the cheap beer flowing and order some nachos or a cheeseburger to help you get in the spirit. You may even find yourself taking a fan photo with your favorite after the evening's athletics.

2301 S. 7th St., 314-776-4833,
www.saintlouiswrestling.com

PLAY BOCCE BALL
ON THE HILL

The city boasts a tight-knit and intact ethnic neighborhood in The Hill, and you can work off your Italian dinner (see Mangia and Market on the Hill, page 126) with a match of bocce ball at Milo's Bocce Garden. Unless you come from generations of players who've passed down their techniques to you, skip the league play on Monday through Thursday nights after 6 p.m. Open play welcomes all comers, though, and happens daily from 11 a.m. to 6 p.m., Friday and Saturday from 11 a.m. to 10:30 p.m. If you don't know your pallino from a Pabst, find a friendly old-timer to coach you on the finer points.

5201 Wilson Ave., 314-776-0468,
www.milosboccegarden.com

GO BIRD-WATCHING
ON OPENING DAY

The street party to end all street parties, Opening Day for Cardinals baseball season is practically a sanctioned day to play hooky. Make sure you're wearing red so you'll blend into the crowds of office workers, schoolkids, and far-flung fans visiting their holy site. The constituents of Cardinal Nation mass in and around (newly renovated) Kiener Plaza, where food, music, beer, Clydesdales, and general frivolity form a protective bubble around all who enter. Pro tip: if you tell your group to "meet me at the Musial," just remember that thousands of other people have made that same plan.

Early April,
www.cardinals.com

FIND THAT
ONE ELK

In fact, at the 546-acre Lone Elk Park, you'll find him and plenty of his compatriots, along with bison, wild turkeys, deer, turtles, and more, with the more charismatic megafauna fairly likely to mosey up to your car to see if any snacks are in the offing. There's also a three-mile walking trail, if you prefer your nature unfiltered. Staff feed the animals first thing in the morning, so the best time to view the animals is before 8 a.m. (gates are unlocked around 6:30 or 7 a.m.). Unlike many County parks, pets are not allowed here, not even if they are well-behaved and kept in the car.

1 Lone Elk Park Rd., 314-615-7275,
www.stlouisco.com/ParksandRecreation/ParkPages/LoneElk

TIP
While you're there: you're right next door, so fly on over to the World Bird Sanctuary for a unique opportunity to see falcons, owls, hawks, eagles, and more wild birds, in habitat displays and seriously up-close encounters. No charge for either park.

BIKE THE
RIVERFRONT TRAIL

Set out on two wheels to enjoy the best of city cycling, along eleven paved miles hugging the Mississippi River from just north of the Arch, at the Laclede Power Center, to the Old Chain of Rocks Bridge, an impressive bike/pedestrian span across to Illinois. Light industrial uses and natural elements combine to create an unforgettable juxtaposition of the wild and the urban; it's not uncommon to spot wild turkeys along the trail, in season. After your trip, head back down south of the Arch (near Chouteau and Leonor K. Sullivan) to take in the eye-popping graffiti flood wall. It's an ever-changing canvas for spray-paint artists from all over the country.

Laclede Power Center parking at Leonor K. Sullivan Blvd. and Biddle St.,
one mile north of the Arch, 314-436-1324,
www.confluencegreenway.org

TIP

Three miles north of downtown, just past the Merchants Bridge, stop at the Mary Meachum Freedom Crossing, the state's first documented site on the Underground Railroad. It's named for a free woman of color who accompanied a group of runaway slaves seeking passage to Illinois in 1855.

WATCH THE
EAGLES SOAR

Winter's no time for dedicated naturalists to stay indoors; not with the mass migration overhead of flocks of bald eagles heading south along the Mississippi corridor. Some terrific spots to see these magnificent raptors include the Old Chain of Rocks Bridge or the Audubon Center at Riverlands, a birders paradise featuring an educational and interpretive center with outdoor viewing opportunities. Even if you're a novice, the enthusiastic staff and volunteers will pretty much guarantee that you'll see something on the wing: they scan the skies and reset the spotting scopes as needed to keep birds in view. Grab your binoculars and head on out to bag some unusual sightings for your life list. Perhaps this will be your Big Year.

301 Riverlands Way, West Alton, 636-899-0090,
riverlands.audubon.org

ROLL THUNDER— OLD-SCHOOL— ## AT SARATOGA

Saratoga Lanes, in the bowling business since 1916, delightfully combines the improbable (a second-story location? Really? For a bowling alley?) and the familiar (a no-frills, retro-before-retro-was-cool setup) to create a space the whole gang (or family!) will love. Shoot pool at one of the five pool tables while you wait your turn on one of the eight lanes, drink beer at the square bar in the middle of all the action while you shoot pool . . . the possibilities are enticing. Best of all, you get to dust off your manual skills at "bowling math," because there's no electronic scoring: pencil and paper is about as high-tech as it gets here. Smoking is allowed anywhere on the premises, so be prepared.

2725 Sutton Blvd., 314-645-5308,
www.saratogalanes.com

GET DOWN UNDER
ON A CAVE TOUR

Get this: Missouri is sometimes known as "the cave state." No lie! There are 6,300 known and surveyed caves, and at least one (Meramec Caverns) where a recording of Kate Smith singing "God Bless America" warbles out at a critical point in the tour. For your spelunking excursion, we recommend two underground wonders at Onondaga Cave State Park, about eighty-five miles southwest of the city. Onondaga Cave itself offers an easy, under-one-mile stroll along paved walkways, with electric lighting and a tour guide (April 15 through October 16, between 10 a.m. and 4 p.m.). Take it up a notch with a lantern tour of Cathedral Cave, a bit longer and more strenuous (May 15 through September 15, with a more limited daily schedule; call for exact times). Either way, your old friends stalagmites (with a "g" for coming up from the "ground") and stalactites (with a "c" for hanging down from the "ceiling") will be there, along with many other weird and wonderful formations.

7556 Highway H, Leasburg, 573-245-6576,
www.mostateparks.com/park/onondaga-cave-state-park

REVEL IN RIVALRY
ON TURKEY DAY

The "oldest Thanksgiving Day football rivalry west of the Mississippi" carries on, as it has every Turkey Day since 1907, between the high school Kirkwood Pioneers and the Webster Groves Statesmen. The game is at high noon on the appointed Thursday, with the 400-pound Frisco Bell awarded to the winner, and the consolation prize—the Centennial Brown Jug—going to the losing school. Families have had generations on the field and in the stands, so get your ticket early if you're planning to carpetbag in for the main event.

The game's location alternates, with Kirkwood High School hosting in odd-numbered years, and Webster Groves High School taking evens.

TIP
Of the slate of festivities, on both sides, leading up to the big game, chili fests on Wednesday night may be the most well attended. Each school offers a bevy of entrants, from amateur and class chilis to school board and professional chef varieties. The winners of the respective "professional" categories go head-to-head to be crowned the winner of the coveted Chili Bowl.

TAKE A TWIRL
AT STEINBERG RINK

Under the twinkling lights, tucked beneath the urban bustle of the Central West End, Steinberg Rink provides the backdrop for an almost-storybook winter experience: outdoor ice skating in one of the nation's largest public parks. Stop by the fire pit to toast cold hands and feet, or take a break and watch the action from the indoor/outdoor café. When you are ready, resume gliding gracefully on your rental skates, belly warmed by hot cocoa, hand warmed by the hand of your beloved, heart warmed by a city that would provide you this moment.

In Forest Park, 400 Jefferson Dr., 314-367-7465,
www.steinbergskatingrink.com

HIKE THE GLADES
AT SHAW NATURE RESERVE

Take in the prairie and marvel at the springtime return of life to the woodlands. These landscapes reveal themselves within the nearly 2,500-acre Shaw Nature Reserve, at the juncture of several of the Midwest's diverse habitats. Spectacular wildlife viewing opportunities, plus trails overlooking the Meramec River, make every season Shaw season. Critters from snakes and herons to beavers and birds all find space to roam. Along Brush Creek Trail, a reproduction sod house lets visitors see a typical Plains settler home of the mid-1800s. If you need an overview that doesn't involve much hiking, the Wilderness Wagon offers a motorized trail ride on Saturday and Sunday afternoons in May and October. And the biennial Prairie Day is a fantastic way to bring the daily activities of early prairie settlers alive.

Highway 100 and I-44, Gray Summit, 636-451-3512,
www.shawnature.org

Compton Hill Water Tower
Credit: Amanda Doyle

CULTURE AND HISTORY

GO UNDER
THE RADAR

Looking for something a bit more unusual than the typical museum visit? St. Louis offers a trio of possibilities for niche audiences. First, two aimed at the kiddo demographic. At HealthWorks! Kids' Museum, your kids can go ape clambering about on the Interactive Dude, an enormous, cross-sectioned body whose ribs, legs, heart, and other parts are just made to explore. A play garden and market teach about healthy nutrition choices, and (in a nod to its origins as a dental museum), there's a massive mouth where kids can practice their brushing and flossing techniques. For kids with sensory disorders and autism spectrum behaviors, We Rock the Spectrum indoor gym provides a plethora of engaging physical activities, including trampolines, swings for all abilities, a small zipline, and more—all in a safe and supportive environment. Finally, for a more adult experience, just nerd *completely* out at the Karpeles Manuscript Museum, one of 14 locations across the country displaying portions of the world's largest privately owned collection of original manuscripts and documents. Thrill to the original landing document of Charles Lindbergh's historic flight to Le Bourget airfield, or pore over the handwritten marginalia in Mark Twain's drafts of *The Adventures of Tom Sawyer.* Exhibits rotate frequently, and special events accompany each new arrival.

⬤ ⬤

HealthWorks!
1100 Macklind Ave., 314-241-7391,
www.hwstl.org

We Rock the Spectrum
2075 Bentley Plaza Dr. in Fenton, 636-529-8282,
www.werockthespectrumfentonmo.com

Karpeles Manuscript Museum
3524 Russell Blvd., 314-282-0234,
www.rain.org/~karpeles

DOUBLE DOWN
ON FALL FUN

They're smart, these city dwellers. By putting on the Best of Missouri Market (at the Missouri Botanical Garden) and the Historic Shaw Art Fair (across the street in the Shaw neighborhood) on the same fall-licious weekend, they figured they'd capitalize on all the handcrafted, local art, and artisan-loving folks who'd naturally be drawn to either event on its own. The result? At least a weekend's worth of exceptional local/national/international art, crafts, furniture, foodstuffs, and entertainment in a beautiful setting, no matter how you split your days. Special shout-out here to the cow-milking station at the Best of Missouri Market: That's a can't-miss photo op. Separate admission fees apply for each event.

First full weekend of October

Missouri Botanical Garden:
4344 Shaw Blvd., 314-577-5100,
www.missouribotanicalgarden.org

Historic Shaw Art Fair:
4100 and 4200 blocks of Flora Place, 314-773-3101,
www.shawartfair.org

TRAVEL THE GLOBE
AT FESTIVAL OF NATIONS

And eat all its foods. It's kind of cliché to say that many people save up calories all year just to chow down on the amazing international cuisines available at the weekend-long Festival of Nations, but there are so many tempting treats that it's hard not to want to binge. Step away from the fry bread, kebabs, and samosas for a few moments, and you'll find the cultural offerings pretty filling, too: music, dance, crafts, cultural demonstrations (like a World Sports and Game Meadow), merchandise (like kids' toys, instruments, alpaca wool sweaters, martial arts equipment), and so much more. The Global Corner, sponsored by the St. Louis Sister Cities Program, educates and builds connections between locals and our 15 sister cities, from Bologna, Italy, to Wuhan, China.

Late August, in Tower Grove Park,
2710 S. Grand Blvd., 314-773-9090,
www.festivalofnationsstl.org

THINK BIG THOUGHTS
AT THE ASSEMBLY SERIES

The presence of several high-quality universities in St. Louis means a wealth of opportunities that can enrich the entire community—but only if the community finds out and takes advantage! Prime example? The Assembly Series of speakers at Washington University. For more than half a century, the school has organized lectures from well-known and highly regarded thinkers, writers, artists, and other influential folks to offer programs, free and open to the public, on some of the day's most important issues. From scientists to documentary filmmakers, from musicians to agents of historical change, it's an education you'd do well to acquire. Bonus: Frequently the lectures are held at the lovely Graham Chapel, as inspirational a setting as you'd hope to enjoy.

One Brookings Dr., 314-935-4620,
assemblyseries.wustl.edu

ALL ABOARD!
WABASH FRISCO AND PACIFIC RAILROAD

Want to blow your toddler's mind? If your wee ones (or for that matter, your father-in-law) loves everything about trains, a half-hour ride in the woods aboard an honest-to-goodness steam engine—albeit a small, 12-gauge one, meaning it's akin to sitting on a moving ottoman—will give them plenty to ooh and aah over. Plan for a short wait in line, the hiss and pop of the wood-fired engine, the shrill whistle echoing in the air, and the scenic riverbank views you'll all remember. Dress for the weather, as you'll be rocking along in the open air. Make an afternoon of it by stopping at the Glencoe City Park after your ride, for climbing and sliding fun.

109 Grand Ave., Glencoe, 636-587-3538,
www.wfprr.com

WADDLE
THE ZOO

The ever-entertaining king and gentoo penguins waddle on their wintertime Sunday walkabouts (weather permitting, of course . . . only in this case, the colder, the better!) While other, more tropical animals might eschew the chill, these birds are completely at ease, loosed from their interior habitat to parade from the nearby gift shop to Penguin & Puffin Coast's entrance, with enchanted visitors snapping photos and marching alongside. If you've ever avoided the inside exhibit because the fishy smell overwhelmed you, here's your ideal viewing opportunity, out in the fresh air of Forest Park! Sundays at 2 p.m. from early December through early February.

One Government Dr., 314-781-0900,
www.stlzoo.org

TRICK OR TREAT
THE CWE

If you're not from these parts, you'll soon discover that Halloween is serious business in St. Louis. Many folks will actually expect their trick-or-treaters to come prepared with a joke or other payment for that candy, and as with many other formerly-reserved-for-kids phenomena, the grownups have horned in on the fun a bit. For a daylong observance of the holiday that candy built, hit the Central West End on the Saturday prior to Halloween: late morning, there's a children's parade and trick-or-treating throughout the neighborhood's streets, and after lunch, a costumed pet parade. Then after the kids hit the sugar-high wall and are tucked away with visions of cavities dancing in their heads, the same streets are taken over by costumed (and often, drunken) adults competing for cash prizes in a costume contest and enjoying the food, drinks, and other hijinks offered by the local bars and restaurants.

At the intersection of Maryland and Euclid Aves.,
www.thecwe.org/events/cwe-halloween

WATCH SPRING EXPLODE
AT PURINA FARMS

Spring hasn't sprung until your wee lambs have held onto a squirming piglet, or stroked a downy chick, or milked a cow, or gotten their snapshot taken with Peter Cottontail; in short, spring really starts at Purina Farms. The annual Springtime Village extravaganza cries out for visits from family groups of all ages, and like so many good things in St. Louis, it's free (reservations required).

Last two weeks of March; days and times vary, 314-982-3232,
38 miles west of St. Louis on Highway MM in Gray Summit,
www.purinafarms.com

TIP
During the Springtime Village event or any other visit, the dog agility and trick shows (held two to three times a day) are a don't-miss. Nothing amazes and amuses like canines hell-bent on getting that Frisbee, even if it means a long leap into the splash pool. Frequent breed shows are a great way to meet up with every kind of pup, from Afghan Hounds to Yorkies.

GET YOUR GOAT
AT GRANT'S FARM

The goats at Grant's Farm have marauded among generations of St. Louis children; why should yours (or you) be any different? Watch as delight turns to abject horror when the wee ones enter the arena with milk bottles at the ready. These cloven-hooved bandits have no decency. Make no mistake: they'd as soon eat you as look at you. OK, probably not. But adult males, especially, should take care to protect themselves. Turns out some vital organs are right about head-butting level. Elsewhere in the parklike wonderland, things get a little more docile, and an elephant show, pony and camel rides, and the world-famous Budweiser Clydesdales all make excellent photo opportunities.

10501 Gravois Rd., 314-843-1700,
www.grantsfarm.com

TIP
Pony up a little more than $200 (for a group of twelve or fewer) and take the Grant's Farm Private Expedition. A private vehicle safari through Deer Park, with hand-feeding of animals and fish, and a visit to the Clydesdale stables are among the highlights. Call 314-525-0829 for scheduling info.

PARADE WITH A PURPOSE
FOR ANNIE MALONE

This town loves a parade! The May Day Parade is a 100-plus-year tradition that's intertwined with the African American community here and across the state, and is among the most joyous and entertaining events to kick off the summer. With floats, marching bands, dance troupes, and step crews, the parade is a showcase and benefit for the Annie Malone Children and Family Service Center, a longstanding center for social services, educational programming, and advocacy for abused, neglected, and abandoned kids. Long held in the historic Ville neighborhood, its fans followed the parade when it moved to the more visible downtown route; a friendlier crowd you'd be hard-pressed to find.

May, starts at 20th & Market, 314-531-0120,
www.anniemalone.com

PICK APPLES
AT ECKERT'S

What could be more wholesome? Head for the mother ship—and add on a hayride, mini-golf, push-pedal tractors, petting zoo, and more—at Eckert's Belleville Farm. In addition to the field and farm fun, there's an enormous market featuring their own produce and great finds from baked goods to jams, specialty candies to teas, and much more. Of course, all that fresh country air will probably work up your appetite, so head on into the country restaurant for a hearty meal, but save room for a stop at the custard stand for dessert. And if it's not apple season? Not to worry. There are u-pick schedules for blackberries, peaches, and pumpkins, too, along with cut-your-own Christmas trees.

951 S. Green Mount Rd., Belleville, IL, 618-233-0513,
www.eckerts.com

SEEK OUT
THE CLASSIC MAGIC

Nothing against the newish digs at the Magic House, but trust me on this: Kids will actually get a kick out of climbing the tucked-away stairs up to what now qualifies as the "old" part of the interactive children's museum, where a certain threadbare charm still captivates. Up in the garret rooms, the pneumatic tube, Bernoulli balls, shadow wall, multi-story slide, and the iconic Van de Graaff generator (a.k.a. the hair-raising metallic orb) still delight. Weirdest find in the attic? An itty-bitty side room with a diminutive table, tea set, and Raggedy Ann and Andy dolls and reading primers. Because it takes a bit of effort to discover, this area is a welcome respite from the more crowded (but still fun!) Children's Village and Beanstalk climber.

516 S. Kirkwood Rd., 314-822-8900,
www.magichouse.org

COMMUNE WITH THE FOREBEARS
AT BELLEFONTAINE CEMETERY

The powers that be at Bellefontaine Cemetery know that sedate and stodgy isn't going to get them anywhere. They'd prefer you come and see the resting places of some of the folks—famous, infamous, and everything in between—who put St. Louis on the map. Monthly second-Saturday tours, along with special themed tours including "Beer Barons" and "Women of Note," will reveal the sometimes-spectacular permanent residences of folks from Adolphus Busch to Sara Teasdale.

Nestled next door to Bellefontaine is the Catholic counterpart, Calvary Cemetery, where the list of prominent people have found their final resting places here includes René Auguste Chouteau, William Tecumseh Sherman, Tennessee Williams, Kate Chopin, and Dred Scott. Let the history lessons begin.

Bellefontaine: 4947 W. Florissant Ave., 314-381-0750,
bellefontainecemetery.org

Calvary: 5239 W. Florissant Ave., 314-792-7738,
archstl.org/cemeteries/content/view/91/233/

PLAY (ON) THE PONIES
AT FAUST PARK

Or the reindeer, or winged griffin-esque creatures . . . at the St. Louis Carousel. Kids and adults can experience the real deal on the circa-1920 merry-go-round, relocated here from its beloved original location at the Forest Park Highlands Amusement Park. Vigorous musical accompaniment by the Stinson Band Organ makes the $2/spin a great deal. Worth a mention is the unusual carousel- and music-box-themed gift shop.

In Faust Park, 15189 Olive Blvd., 314-615-8383,
www.stlouisco.com/ParksandRecreation/ParkPages/Faust

TIP

If it happens to be March, nothing fights the gloom of those last winter days like the thousands of vibrant, near-metallic Blue Morpho peleides butterflies that fill the Butterfly House next door to the Carousel during March Morpho Mania, daily from 9 a.m. to 4 p.m. all month long.

Circus Flora
Credit: David Lancaster

TASTE THE SAWDUST
AT CIRCUS FLORA

It's worth starting a summer circus tradition with your own family, and there's no better place than at the charming, one-ring wonder under the classic red-and-white-striped big top in Grand Center. For nearly a month, the parking lot behind Powell Hall is overtaken by high-wire daredevils, aerialists, jugglers, acrobats, fast-paced and funny animal acts, and one irrepressible clown. It's a circus in the style of classical, European troupes, with generations of family performers. You can sit close enough to have the sawdust fly in your lap from the pounding horses' hooves, if that's your thing. Live music makes the experience even more magical, and the very personal touch lasts all the way through the exit, when you can meet and talk to all the performers as you leave the tent.

Grand Blvd. and Samuel Shepard Dr., 314-289-4040,
www.circusflora.org

GO GREEN
AT DOGTOWN'S
ST. PATRICK'S DAY PARADE

One of the several proud waves of immigrants who came early and plentifully to these Mississippi shores, the Irish (and would-be Irish) of St. Louis maintain a lively presence felt most keenly around St. Patrick's Day, when both a proper downtown parade and a neighborhood-based celebration draw crowds. Get the most authentic flavor at the Dogtown parade, held on the day itself down Tamm Avenue, workdays and weekdays be damned. From floats bearing dancers to families and friends marching under their clan's heritage crest, it's a family-friendly (if a bit raucous) good time.

TIP

Following the lead of Mardi Gras, no coolers are allowed into the neighborhood on parade day. Save yourself time and possible ticketing and park in the Zoo's south lot. You can easily get to the parade by walking over the Tamm Ave. bridge to Dogtown. Join the hardy crowd for pre-parade breakfast at Pat Connolly's Tavern.

GET MOVING
AT THE MUSEUM OF TRANSPORTATION

The Museum of Transportation exerts an almost physical pull on both transportation-obsessed schoolkids and their Baby Boom-or-older grandfathers. You can see it in their eyes as they wander the outdoor tracks loaded with historic locomotives, trolley cars, and streetcars, or inside showrooms displaying classic cars and aircraft. More than seventy locomotives—many the sole surviving examples of their type—are on display, but what will really move you are the streetcar and miniature train rides.

Auto buffs will enjoy the St. Louis Motor Carriage automobile, produced in 1901; the Bobby Darin custom "Dream Car," built in 1960; a 1963 Chrysler Turbine Car, the only operational model on public display in the world; and other interesting cars and trucks. For the landlocked, clambering about the decks of the H.T. Pott tugboat moored out front will provide plenty of fun.

3015 Barrett Station Rd., 314-965-6212,
www.transportmuseumassociation.org

TIP
Spend the extra $2 per person for the children in your group to spend an hour inside Creation Station, a fun, hands-on space where they can play, dress up, craft, crawl, and generally unwind. It's air-conditioned, which on hot days will be well worth the extra bucks for the adults, too. The Station, however, is closed to the public on weekends, to allow for private parties.

CRUISE
THE RIVER

For the best views of the downtown skyline, you've got to get a little distance, say from the deck of the replica paddle-wheel steamboats *Becky Thatcher* and *Tom Sawyer,* as they take a one-hour sightseeing tour, offered several times daily for most of the year. Or put a different twist on it with one of the popular nighttime blues cruises, featuring live music from stellar local musicians, drinks and dancing, and the bright lights of the big city. Specialty cruises, including Halloween, New Year's Eve, and a Kimmswick shopping tour, are offered as well.

50 S. Leonor K. Sullivan Blvd., 877-982-1410,
www.gatewayarch.com

TAKE A SPIN
ON THE ROOFTOP FERRIS WHEEL

There's run-of-the-mill wacky, and then there's City Museum–grade wacky. The fantastical, industrial, recycled playspace—full of tunnels and slides and a shoelace factory—that was the brainchild of artist Bob Cassilly achieves its apex, appropriately, up on the roof. A school bus dangles off one corner, appearing to lurch precariously off the building, and slides of varying levels of thrill are scattered about. But you're already this high, so why not add four more stories to it? Stand in line to ride Big Eli, the restored Ferris wheel that, in temperate months, takes you up to an unparalleled view of the city.

701 N. 15th St., 314-231-CITY,
www.citymuseum.org

Cahokia Mounds interpretive center
Credit: Amanda Doyle

CELEBRATE SOLSTICE
AT CAHOKIA MOUNDS

Our very own backyard (well, Southern Illinois, anyway) boasts a UNESCO World Heritage Site—meaning if you haven't made it to the pre-Columbian, Native American–built metropolis of Cahokia Mounds, it's like skipping out on the Great Wall of China or the Taj Mahal. For what, so you could sleep in? Set the alarm and hightail it to the summer—or winter—solstice celebration at the site's Woodhenge solar calendar, to welcome the dawn with a small but hardy bunch of your fellow homo sapiens. An archaeologist will be on hand to explain the discovery and function of the Woodhenge posts, used in Cahokia's heyday to mark the solstices and other sacred days.

30 Ramey St., Collinsville, IL, 618-346-5160,
cahokiamounds.org

RELIVE ST. LOUIS'S VICTORIAN HEYDAY
AT THE CAMPBELL HOUSE

An afternoon at downtown's Campbell House steeps you in the culture and trappings of the 1880s, through the remarkably restored mansion of Robert Campbell (built in 1851), a rough-and-tumble frontier fur trader who traded in that life (mostly) to become a pillar of civilized society. The home contains hundreds of original possessions, furnishings, artwork, letters, and more belonging to the family—something of a rarity in a historic home—and shows how the city grew into its role as the Gateway to the West in a young, optimistic country. The building was the first house built in a then-elegant, new neighborhood, and now remains the lone freestanding residential sentinel on the block.

1508 Locust St., 314-421-0325,
www.campbellhousemuseum.org

EXPERIENCE HOLY AWE
AT THE BASILICA

Awe is the natural reaction in the remarkable presence of the world's largest collection of mosaic art under one (big) roof, at the Cathedral Basilica. Walls and ceilings tell stories of Christ, Catholicism, and the affairs of the Church and its mission in the local area. The events of the life of King Louis IX, our city's (and the cathedral's) namesake, are depicted in the narthex. A fascinating mosaic museum in the basement demonstrates the marriage of artistry and precision required to make the vision a reality.

4431 Lindell Blvd., 314-373-8241,
www.cathedralstl.org

TIP
If you want an expert to show you the highlights, call ahead for a tour reservation, available weekdays from 10 a.m. to 4 p.m. Sunday tours, following noon Mass, don't need a reservation.

"Four, five, six! chimed the clock, and Cinderella ran as she had never run before."

CINDERELLA

EXPLORE
CENTRAL LIBRARY

Following a meticulous $70 million renovation that touched on everything from interior lights to relocating literally tons of volumes, the flagship downtown branch of the St. Louis Public Library wows anew with soaring public spaces, an inviting and interactive kids' wing, the inspiring "St. Louis Room," a main-floor café, spiffy new auditorium space (where the coal bin once lived), and much more. This ain't your grandpa's library . . . but bring him along for the fun! And it's not just local boosters who have noticed the spiffy restoration. In early 2013, the reborn library won the popular vote in the Architizer A+ Library Award, an international competition.

1301 Olive St., 314-241-2288,
www.slpl.org

GET HIGH
AT THE COMPTON HILL WATER TOWER

Up 198 steps you'll find yourself at the top of the 170-foot French Romanesque Compton Hill Water Tower, as elegant a shell as was ever constructed to conceal a 100-foot standpipe. Built in 1898, the tower offers 360-degree views as far as Illinois and the Jefferson Barracks Bridge. It is open the first Saturday of each month from April to November, from noon to 4 p.m., as well as on the evenings of full moons during those months. The park below is a pleasant place to stroll and ponder "The Naked Truth," a massive bronze and stone statue of a naked woman holding torches to symbolize the enlightenment of the United States and Germany, the home country of its sculptor and the men it memorializes.

In Compton Hill Reservoir Park, Grand & Russell Blvds., 314-552-9000, www.watertowerfoundation.org

REMEMBER RAGTIME
AT SCOTT JOPLIN'S HOUSE

Scott Joplin, the king of ragtime, spent some of his most productive years living with his wife in a second-floor flat in St. Louis where he wrote some of his most famous works, including "Elite Syncopations" and "The Entertainer." Today, it's preserved as the Scott Joplin House State Historic Site, and you'll hear his melodies on a player piano as you tour the home.

2658A Delmar Blvd., 314-340-5790,
www.mostateparks.com/scottjoplin.htm

TIP
Want a modern-day ragtime experience?
The Friends of Scott Joplin organization hosts a rollicking
Ragtime Rendezvous at 5:30 p.m. the first Sunday of each month at the
new Rosebud Café, adjacent to the historic home.
See www.friendsofscottjoplin.org for details.

ACKNOWLEDGE MOM'S ARTFUL PARENTING
AT LAUMEIER

Forgot to make reservations for brunch? No problem! The sunshine, fresh air, and truly lovely surroundings of the annual Mother's Day art fair at Laumeier Sculpture Park will make you Mom's favorite child. Excellent curated fine art and crafts from around the nation, plus music and wine tasting, will make mom even happier than a nap. Well, at least as happy as a nap. And you will get credit for having thought of it!

Mother's Day Weekend, 12580 Rott Rd., 314-615-5278,
www.laumeiersculpturepark.org

TIP
Missed Mother's Day?
Several other high-quality art fairs are worth the browse. In Belleville, the annual Art on the Square fair happens the weekend after Mother's Day. The Saint Louis Art Fair, in Clayton, is a cherished annual tradition for many in September. And Art Outside, hosted by Schlafly Bottleworks, takes a different tack on the same September weekend, highlighting affordable art and crafts from exclusively local makers.

Art on the Square
800-677-9255,
www.artonthesquare.com

Saint Louis Art Fair
314-863-0278,
www.culturalfestivals.com

Art Outside
314-241-2337, ext. 252,
www.schlafly.com/events

GO TO THE TOP
OF THE GATEWAY ARCH

Seriously. Just go, already. You have my permission. You don't even need an out-of-towner. It's an engineering and architectural marvel, built by fearless visionaries, and it means "St. Louis" to the world.

St. Louis Riverfront, 877-982-1410,
www.gatewayarch.com

EXPLORE MISSOURI'S
AFRICAN AMERICAN HISTORY

From Africans brought across the Middle Passage during the slave trade to Dred and Harriet Scott, whose appeal for their freedom and rights shook the world, to Madame C. J. Walker, widely acknowledged as America's first self-made female millionaire, the influence of prominent and ordinary black citizens on our state—and indeed, on the world—is both profound and undersung. At The Griot Museum of Black History, visitors can build on their knowledge of important African American historical figures through artifacts, life-size wax figures, and traveling exhibits. Special events and a shop add to the experience.

2505 St. Louis Ave., 314-241-7057,
www.thegriotmuseum.com

SPOOK YOURSELF
AT LEMP MANSION

The much-put-upon Lemp family of St. Louis brewing fame experienced more than its fair share of depression, suicide, and unexplained death. But misery loves entrepreneurship, and the folks at the Lemp Mansion have turned those hardships into an entertaining adventure with "the Lemp Experience," a ghost-hunting/supernatural investigatory tour of the property that includes drinks and appetizers. You can even book an overnight stay to put your interest in the paranormal to the ultimate test.

3322 DeMenil Place, 314-664-8024,
www.lempmansion.com

MARCH INTO HISTORY
AT JEFFERSON BARRACKS

During World War II Weekend, the public is invited to stroll the grounds of Jefferson Barracks Park, where re-enactors representing U.S., British, Canadian, Soviet, and German troops of the period are camped. The re-enactors educate visitors about their uniforms, weapons, and equipment. Battle re-enactments give an up-close and personal view of the warfare of the period, and kids are allowed to gather spent shell casings as souvenirs after the smoke clears.

Last weekend of April, 345 North Rd., 314-615-5270,
stlouisco.com/ParksandRecreation/ParkPages/JeffersonBarracks

TIP
Ages 18 and up can enjoy a typical
World War II "canteen dance" with a visiting Big Band
on Saturday night. Brush up on your swing moves!

CHANNEL YOUR INNER
ARCHITECT

The Frank Lloyd Wright House in Ebsworth Park (that's FLWHEP to you) provides a pristine example of the aesthetic of the renowned architect, right down to the original furniture and fabrics he designed for the home's interior. It was the first home Wright built in St. Louis, and is one of just five of his designs in the state. Wright felt middle-class Americans should be able to afford beautiful architecture: he was determined to show it in places like Kirkwood. Tours of the Kirkwood site are by appointment only, Wednesday to Sunday.

120 N. Ballas Rd., 314-822-8359,
www.ebsworthpark.org

CELEBRATE THE SEASON
AT THE OLD COURTHOUSE

Holiday majesty doesn't get much more handsome digs than the rotunda of the historic Old Courthouse, in the shadow of the Gateway Arch. Typically starting the day after Thanksgiving, a revolving cast of invited performers—everything from brass quintets to children's choirs—offers free noontime concerts of Christmas and other holiday music. Opportunities for singalong caroling in the authentic Victorian décor—less ostentatious than we've gotten in modern times—can't help but warm the heart.

11 N. 4th St., 314-655-1614,
www.coreofdiscovery.com

KNOW
YOUR RIVER

For a great overview of both the cultural and historical importance of the Big Muddy to the actual logistics of modern management of a very busy commercial waterway, trek to the Melvin Price Locks & Dam and the National Great Rivers Museum. Tour interactive exhibits, try your hand at captaining a model barge, and hike up eighty feet to overlook barges moving through the brilliant lock system. At the museum, two film features explore "The Power of the River" and "The Mississippi River Water Trail." An education worth any price—and for each experience, the price happens to be "free."

#1 Lock and Dam Way, East Alton, IL, 877-462-6979

NA ZDROWIE!

Pronounced "nahs-drove-yah," it means "to your health!" a phrase that'll come in handy at the Polish Festival organized in the fall by the members of the Polish Falcons Nest 45, a fraternal organization that maintains a stately mansion HQ in North St. Louis. Prepare to polka, of course, and also to enjoy some fine home cooking, imported beer, live music, and the unstoppable pride of the Poles. This event draws people back to the neighborhood where many of their parents and grandparents lived, even if the current generation maintains no other direct connection.

September, 2013 St. Louis Ave., 314-421-9614

TIP

Want to explore more cultures with a presence in the metro area? Check out the St. Nicholas Greek Festival (Labor Day Weekend), Italian Fest in Collinsville (September), and Deutsch Country Days in October.

Greek Festival, 4967 Forest Park Blvd., 314-361-6924, www.sngoc.org

Italian Fest, 221 W. Main St., Collinsville, IL, 618-344-2884, www.italianfest.net

Deutsch Country Days, 18055 State Highway O, Marthasville, 636-433-5669, www.deutschcountrydays.org

TAKE YOUR MAMA FOR SOME DRAMA
AT THE SHAKESPEARE FESTIVAL

Or perhaps one of the comedies? Depending on the year, the Shakespeare Festival of St. Louis might be performing any of the playwright's timeless works, but whether you lean more toward the tragic or comedic, the theatergoer in you will be utterly enchanted by the outing. Free outdoor productions by professional actors are presented on a full stage nestled in a sylvan glade in Forest Park (the east side of Art Hill, now dubbed "Shakespeare Glen"). Food and drink are available for purchase, and on a summer night with a loaf of bread, a jug of wine, and the company of your fellow citizens, you can achieve Bardic bliss.

In Forest Park, May-June, 314-531-9800,
www.sfstl.com

TIP

Rental chairs are available if lounging on your own blanket is not your thing. Arrive between 5:30 and 8:00 for first-come, first-served options. You should aim to arrive by 6:30 anyway, as that's the kickoff time for the nightly Green Show, featuring jugglers, singers, and a short preview of the show.

SWOON FOR A
SUMMER NIGHT

Make like old times, and point your vehicle east for a double feature at the Skyview Drive-In. You pay, you park, you watch a feature film or two on the big screen under the stars. One upgrade that has taken place since days of yore: Instead of a speaker slung over each car's window, the movie's sound is now transmitted via FM radio. Tickets are cash only (about $10/person, with two kids free with each paying adult), and, although they have a full menu at the concession stand, bringing your own food and drink is allowed, so plan ahead. Alcohol is allowed for patrons who are of legal age to drink it. Want to bring lawn chairs, blankets, a bucket of chicken, and your dog? No problem. It's the rare treat that lives up to its fun factor in your memory: luckily, this is one.

5700 North Belt West, Belleville, IL, 618-233-4400,
www.skyview-drive-in.com

FIND YOUR ZEN
AT THE JAPANESE FESTIVAL

At more than thirty-five years old, this annual Labor Day Weekend gathering is one of the oldest in the United States devoted to exploring the history, culture, and people of Japan—a milestone that makes sense when you consider the special relationship the Missouri Botanical Garden has had with Japan since the dedication of its Japanese Garden, Seiwa-en, in 1977. From ikebana (the Japanese art of flower arranging) and impressive taiko drumming to exclusive Teahouse Island tours and tea ceremonies, the weekend is a kaleidoscope of sights, sounds, and experiences visitors won't soon forget.

Labor Day Weekend, 4344 Shaw Blvd., 314-577-5100,
www.missouribotanicalgarden.org

TIP
Available spots (twenty per tour) for the teahouse tour are snapped up quickly, so send someone from your party to stand in line if that's one of your priorities. Tickets are $5 each (cash only, max of four per person), and sold twice daily at the Plum Viewing Arbor. Tickets go on sale one hour before the first scheduled tour of each daily set and are sold for all tours in that set. Check the website at festival time to find each day's set times.

SHARE A SECRET
AT UNION STATION

Take someone trustworthy to the northern entrance of Union Station's Grand Hall, and position yourselves on each end of the entrance arch, with backs to each other. The sweet nothings (or juicy somethings) you utter to the Whispering Arch will travel right over. Then, head up to the comfy seating areas and enjoy a bite (or maybe a train-themed cocktail) while you take in the immersive sights and sounds of the state-of-the-art 3D projections on the domed ceiling.

1820 Market St., 314-231-1234,
www.stlouisunionstation.com

FAIRE-THEE-WELL
AT THE ST. LOUIS RENAISSANCE FAIRE

Get a feel for life in a sixteenth-century English village, as represented through this annual festival re-enacting the song, dance, jousting, shopping, crafts, and entertainment of the era. Volunteer villagers take on the roles of peasants, nobility, knights, and ne'er-do-wells while professional acting and singing troupes perform and entertain. A special Kids' Kingdom teaches more about the customs of the time. You are encouraged to come in costume to add to the colorful spectacle that goes far beyond with themed weekends, armored jousting, nine stages spread throughout the grounds, and more than 100 artisans hawking their wares. Short demonstrations are offered on such disparate skills as sword-fighting, archery, making chain mail, using a trebuchet, building a fairy house, and of course, there is always "pirate skool." Along with the giant turkey leg concession stand, you can feast on chocolate covered cheesecake on a stick, roasted almonds and pecans at the King's Nuts, and ice cold pickles, as well as more familiar fare at stands and sit-down cafés throughout the faire-grounds. The scavenger hunt will keep the young ones busy for hours. Weekends from mid-September to mid-October.

Rotary Park in Foristell, 636-928-4141,
www.stlrenfest.com

HIT THE HAY
AT FAUST PARK

Clamber on up to the flatbed trailer and stake your spot on a hay bale for a fall ride through Faust Park, which includes a stop or two for brief talks showcasing the park's historic significance. Then clamber back down and spend a few minutes or hours exploring the candlelit village's restored buildings. A working blacksmith shop, a re-enacted prairie funeral with wailing mourners, and a one-room schoolhouse are among the highlights. Samples of period-authentic refreshments like gingersnaps and cider are served, and ample entertainment is provided by the live folk music and raging bonfires. Advance reservations are required.

15185 Olive Blvd., 314-615-8328,
www.stlouisco.com/ParksandRecreation/ParkPages/Faust

UNEARTH RECENT
MISSOURI HISTORY

Get a fascinating glimpse into the postwar decades in St. Louis, with exhibits examining suburban growth and land use patterns, playgrounds and neighborhood identity, civil rights protests and sit-ins, the role of professional baseball in the city's community life, significant writers and musicians from the area, and many more national and local topics in the Missouri History Museum's Reflections Gallery. Plenty of hands-on exhibits make this an especially kid-friendly corner: they especially like trying out the playground games of generations past, and watching the maps of changing housing patterns light up.

5700 Lindell Blvd., 314-746-4599,
www.mohistory.org

TIP
More Local Lore

A handful of niche collections, open to the public, can shed further light on our history. At the Lutheran Church–Missouri Synod's International Center, a museum dedicated to preserving and sharing the history of Lutheranism in America, exhibits examine everything from the denomination's heritage and growth to its proliferation in our area. The Mercantile Library, the oldest library west of the Mississippi, is a trove of documents, artifacts, and art related to Westward Expansion and St. Louis history and prehistory. And the St. Louis Soccer Hall of Fame preserves the stories and memorabilia of the sport's parks, heroes, leagues, and highlights.

Concordia Historical Institute Museum
1333 S. Kirkwood Rd., 314-505-7900,
www.lutheranhistory.org

Mercantile Library
7606 Natural Bridge Rd. (at UMSL), 314-516-7248,
www.umsl.edu/mercantile

St. Louis Soccer Hall of Fame
5247 Fyler Ave., 314-781-8493,
www.eteamz.com/stlsoccerhalloffame

FIND YOURSELF
ON THE FRINGE

Unjuried, uncensored, unpredictable, and (in some cases) unpolished: the characteristics that make up a potential Fringe Festival act. A worldwide phenomenon, the Fringe now has a firm foothold in St. Louis, with a nine-day festival in August along with a slate of happenings throughout the rest of the calendar. Actors, dancers, spoken word artists, musicians, improv teams, and many others come together in unique ways to create artistic experiences for their audiences that require much more in the way of collaboration than technical effects or expertise. Love it, hate it, or just puzzled by it? Then Fringe has done its job of engaging you.

Venues in and around Grand Center, 314-643-7853,
www.stlouisfringe.com

HealthWorks! Kids' Museum
Credit: Amanda Doyle

Citygarden
Credit: David Lancaster

NEIGHBORHOODS/PLACES

TOUR THE
TOWN

Ready for some professional help in setting a course for your discoveries? Sign up for a themed tour of an aspect of St. Louis that interests you most. If the way to your heart is through your stomach, both Savor St. Louis and St. Louis Culinary Tours will tempt you. Savor leads walking/tasting tours in The Loop, the Central West End, and Downtown, sprinkling nuggets of history, architectural trivia, and local lore in between generous samplings of some of the best restaurants each neighborhood has to offer. STL Culinary Tours also takes a themed approach, with a gourmet (and pricier) approach to insider foodie knowledge.

Or, if your gustatorial needs are already taken care of, sign on with the irreverent and irrepressible Renegade Tours instead, whose "Central West End for Nerds," "Queer St. Louis," and "Disasters and Catastrophes" itineraries, among others, bring a can't-be-bored sensibility to our architectural and historical legacies.

Savor St. Louis, 866-736-6343,
www.savorsaintlouis.com

STL Culinary Tours,
www.stlculinarytours.com

Renegade Tours, 314-467-8588,
www.renegadestl.com

STROLL DOWN
CANDY CANE LANE

Not a creation of Willie Wonka, but an actual residential street in the St. Louis Hills neighborhood, the 6500 block of Murdoch transforms itself, via thousands of lights and countless hours of neighbor-labor, into a twinkling wonderland of Christmas cheer. For about a decade, the residents here have been inviting visitors in and collecting donations for area charities. They've been so successful that adjacent blocks have joined in the fun, too. Check out Angel Avenue (4700 block of Prague Ave.) and Snow Flake Street (6500 block of Neosho St.).

6500 block of Murdoch Ave., St. Louis Hills

TIP
Rather than idling in the sometimes-long car line, park around the corner and bundle up for a winter stroll down the block.

LIVE LA VIDA
CHEROKEE

One of the most consistently interesting mashups in town occurs along the length of Cherokee Street, on the city's South Side. A Mexican/Latin American business district offers everything from authentic beef tongue tacos to jerseys from the world's best soccer teams, while artists and cultural creatives have brought everything from letterpress printing and neighborhood-niche T-shirts to handmade art jewelry and hard-to-find music. Spend some time to find your own favorites. Stumped? Start at: La Vallesana, Stylehouse, Earthbound Beer, Flowers to the People, South City Art Supply, Dead Wax, Siete Luminarias, Gooolll, The Firecracker Press, and then on to Teatopia, for a full day that only scratches the surface of this vibrant neighborhood.

www.cherokeestation.com

CLANG,
CLANG, CLANG

Decades in the dreaming and making, a working trolley/streetcar line has been brought back to life by serial entrepreneur Joe Edwards. It's a short recreation of the vast network of streetcars that used to crisscross and connect the city, but the refurbished vintage cars will transport riders back and forth between the History Museum and The Loop, connecting some of the most heavily touristed parts of the central corridor. Planning and construction delays have caused some headaches for those who live and work along the route, so the "ding, ding!" delivering passengers to spots along the tracks is a welcome sound, indeed. Fun fact: the three refurbished trolley cars (painted red, blue, and orange, respectively) arrived here from a previous life of service in Seattle. See? Pacific Northwest to Midwest migration can happen!

www.looptrolley.com

SPLASH AND STROLL
AT CITYGARDEN

The ultimate "build it, and they will come" project, this interactive sculpture park and water-filled oasis smack dab in the heart of downtown brings together wading kids, sun-seeking escapees from the nearby office high-rises, curious out-of-towners, and the rest of life's rich pageant. Wander among the giant bunnies, sideways head, bird-boy hybrid, and lots of other playful art, while the anxious-looking security guards try to decide how much to rein in the exuberance. BYO sunscreen and blanket, but if you forget the picnic basket, well-stocked food trucks tend to congregate nearby. There's also an outpost of Kaldi's Coffee in the jewelbox of a restaurant overlooking the park.

8th, 9th, and 10th streets, between Market and Chestnut,
www.citygardenstl.org

MANGIA AND MARKET
ON THE HILL

The Hill offers a can't-go-wrong collection of Italian restaurants. A grab bag of three: for the full-on fine-dining experience, Dominic's; for St. Louis Italian-American the way it was popularized, Zia's; for a sleeper hit, Lorenzo's Trattoria. Want to recreate a meal at home? Shop the local markets, stocking up on essentials from imported tomatoes and more pasta shapes than you might've known existed, to hard candies, St. Louis–style pizza fixings, house-cured meats, deli sandwiches, specialty flours and sauces, Italian-themed gifts, kitchen gadgets, and so much more. All products are priced reasonably, even when compared to the big guys! Of several worthy options, the nod here goes to DiGregorio's Market, a clean, well-lighted space where it's nearly impossible to leave empty-handed.

The following streets border the Hill:
Manchester, Hampton, Kingshighway, Southwest, and Columbia

Dominic's
5101 Wilson Ave., 314-771-1632,
www.dominicsrestaurant.com

Lorenzo's Trattoria
1933 Edwards St., 314-773-2223,
www.lorenzostrattoria.com

Zia's
5256 Wilson Ave., 314-776-0020,
www.zias.com

DiGregorio's Market
5200 Daggett Ave., 314-776-1062,
www.digregoriofoods.com

FALL FOR
THE GREAT RIVER ROAD

It's the Mississippi River as you may never have seen it before, all shimmery and glorious in its wildness, with the dramatic limestone bluffs of Alton, Elsah, and Grafton, Illinois, soaring up to its east. For fall foliage peeping, the drive can't be beat. Along the way, make sure to pay respect to the legendary painted Piasa bird just north of Alton. The fearsome man-eater first appeared in prehistoric pictographs and is no less menacing today.

Cross the river at the Clark Bridge at Alton, IL,
www.greatriverroad.com

TIP
The northern terminus of the Great River Road puts you at Pere Marquette State Park, a great spot for breakfast or lunch in its rustic lounge. You can also enjoy giant chess, horseback trail riding, and hiking in the park. www.pmlodge.net

STROLL THE COBBLESTONES
IN HISTORIC ST. CHARLES

Main Street St. Charles aims squarely at the domesticated lady of a certain age, with its charming shops specializing in home décor, collectibles, teapots, Christmas ornaments, and baubles. Even if that's not you, it's a pleasant afternoon admiring the intact, historic business district, popping into the old-fashioned ice cream and candy shops, or settling in with a fresh beer at Trailhead Brewing Company. Stores like Main Street Books and Provenance Soapworks are great examples of thriving independent business along the strip. And there is real history to be found: Both Missouri's first state capitol and the Lewis & Clark Boat House and Nature Center will appeal to buffs. Around Christmas, the Legends of Christmas figures (like Santas from around the world and the Sugarplum Fairy) stroll the street, spreading cheer and handing out their own personalized trading cards.

www.historicstcharles.com

LAUGH AT
OLD MAN WINTER
IN THE LOOP

"There is no bad weather, only unsuitable clothing." Surely that quote, attributed to more than one outdoorsman, was bandied about at the creation of the Loop Ice Carnival, a January weekend of frozen-buns family fun, from ice sculpting and ice slides to fire jugglers and human dog sledders. Businesses up and down Delmar will help you dress appropriately and develop the right mindset for the Midwest winter weather. They offer snacks, special sales, games, and a collection of zany that reminds you why the Loop is good for any reason, in every season.

www.visittheloop.com/about/events

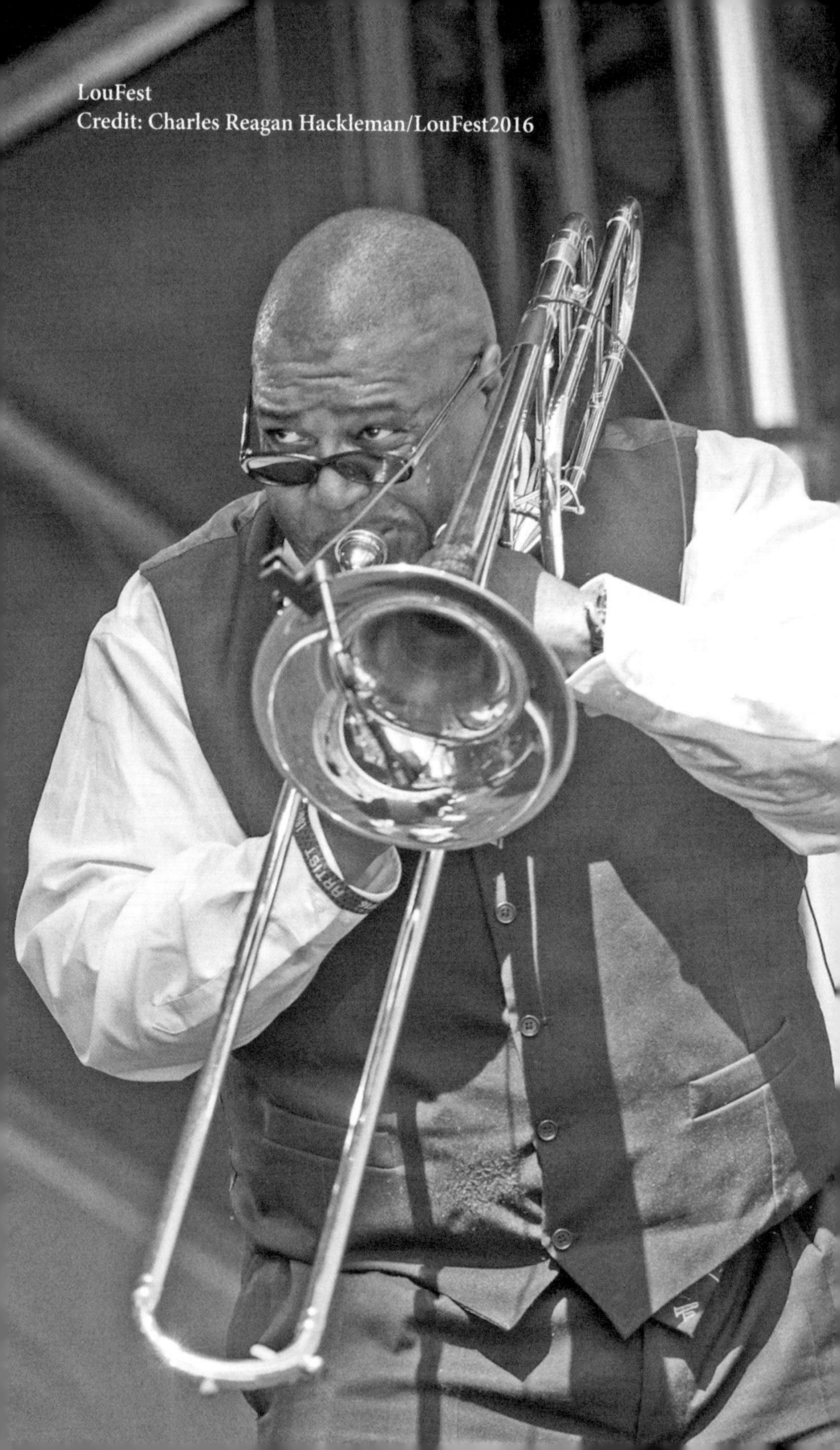

LouFest
Credit: Charles Reagan Hackleman/LouFest2016

SUGGESTED
ITINERARIES

CLASSIC STL TRIFECTA

Anheuser-Busch Brewery Tour, 2

Gateway Arch, 100

Cardinals Opening Day, 56

HITS FOR MUSIC LOVERS

BB's, 28

National Blues Museum, 27

Compton Heights Concert Band, 30

Jazz at the Bistro, 31

Scott Joplin State Historic Site, 97

LouFest, 33

St. Louis Symphony Orchestra, 41

Vintage Vinyl, 39

Whitaker Music Festival, 34

SPORTY SPOTS

Arch Madness, 44

Busch Stadium Tour, 48

Biking the Riverfront Trail, 58

Gateway Cup Bicycle Races, 52

Sailing at Creve Coeur Lake, 51

FOODIE FAVORITES

OFF THE BEATEN PATH

The Loop Trolley
Credit: Courtesy Joe Edwards

ACTIVITIES
BY SEASON

WINTER

Sledding on Art Hill, 45

Christmas Lights on Candy Cane Lane, 121

March Morpho Mania at the Butterfly House, 83

Eagle-watching, 60

Lenten fish fries, 12

The Loop Ice Carnival, 129

Mardi Gras Pet Parade and Wiener Dog Races, 37

Holiday caroling at the Old Courthouse, 105

Ice skating at Steinberg Rink, 64

SPRING

World War II Weekend at Jefferson Barracks, 103

Mother's Day Art Fair at Laumeier Sculpture Park, 98

Annie Malone May Day Parade, 78

Springtime Village at Purina Farms, 76

Hiking at Shaw Nature Reserve, 65

SUMMER

Summer solstice at Cahokia Mounds, 91

STL Fringe Festival, 116

Circus Flora, 85

Splashing at Citygarden, 125

Festival of Nations, 71

FALL

STL Stylehouse on Cherokee Street
Credit: David Lancaster

INDEX

View from Citygarden
Credit: David Lancaster